Maths

National Test Practice Papers

Hilary Koll and Steve Mills

**Age 10–11
Year 6**
Key Stage 2

Contents	Page

Hachette UK's policy is to use papers that are natural, renewable and recyclable products and made from wood grown in sustainable forests. The logging and manufacturing processes are expected to conform to the environmental regulations of the country of origin.

Orders: please contact Bookpoint Ltd, 130 Milton Park, Abingdon, Oxon OX14 4SB. Telephone: (44) 01235 827720. Fax: (44) 01235 400454. Lines are open 9.00a.m.–5.00p.m., Monday to Saturday, with a 24-hour message answering service. Visit our website at www.hoddereducation.co.uk.

© Hilary Koll and Steve Mills 2013
First published in 2008 exclusively for WHSmith by
Hodder Education
An Hachette UK Company
338 Euston Road
London NW1 3BH

This second edition first published in 2013 exclusively for WHSmith by Hodder Education.

Impression number   10 9 8 7 6 5 4 3
Year   2018 2017 2016 2015 2014 2013

Cover illustration by Oxford Designers and Illustrators Ltd
Typeset by DC Graphic Design Ltd, Swanley Village, Kent
Printed in Great Britain by Hobbs the Printers Ltd, Totton, Hampshire SO40 3WX

A catalogue record for this title is available from the British Library.

ISBN: 978 1444 189 186

NOTE: The tests, questions and advice in this book are not reproductions of the official test materials sent to schools. The official testing process is supported by guidance and training for teachers in setting and marking tests and interpreting the results. The results achieved in the tests in this book may not be the same as are achieved in the official tests.

End of Key Stage Assessments

Children who attend state schools in England are assessed at the ages of 7, 11 and 14 as they approach the end of Key Stages 1, 2 and 3 respectively. They are assessed through tasks, tests and by teacher assessments throughout the year. Each child's level is reported to his or her parents/guardians and the collective information about pupils' levels is used to monitor schools.

Key Stage	Year	Age by end of year	National Tests
1 (KS1)	1	6	
	2	7	National Curriculum Statutory tasks and tests
2 (KS2)	3	8	Optional Year 3
	4	9	Optional Year 4
	5	10	Optional Year 5
	6	11	National Curriculum Statutory tasks and tests
3 (KS3)	7	12	Optional Year 7
	8	13	Optional Year 8
	9	14	Optional Year 9

All children in their final year of Key Stage 1 are assessed using the statutory National Curriculum tasks and tests, administered to all eligible children who are working at Level 1 or above in reading, writing and mathematics. Tasks and tests are designed to help inform the final teacher assessment judgement reported for each child at the end of Key Stage 1. These assessments can be carried out at any point during the year up to the end of June.

At the end of **Key Stage 2**, 11-year-olds sit statutory National Curriculum tests during a week in May. In mathematics these include two written papers for children working up to Level 5 and a mental maths test. There is an optional Level 6 test, involving two papers, which exceptionally able children can be submitted for. A Practice Paper for Level 6 is available in this WHSmith range (ISBN 978 1444 189 230). Children may also sit optional tests in the intervening years (Years 3, 4 and 5).

Whilst these WHSmith Practice Papers might not give exactly the same results as national tests or assessments they can give an indication of the child's attainment and progress and highlight any areas that need more practice. More information on levels and how to convert your child's score into a level is found on page 37.

Maths at Key Stage 2

The Key Stage 2 National Tests cover Number, Measures, Shape and Space, and Data Handling. Most children will take two 45-minute written tests and a short, orally delivered mental test. Test A is a written non-calculator paper and Test B is a written paper where children can use a calculator, should they wish to.

Levels

Children taking the Mathematics Tests A and B and the Mental Mathematics Test can achieve below Level 3, Level 3, Level 4 or Level 5, with a typical 11-year-old attaining Level 4.

To gain an idea of the level at which your child is working, use the table on page 37, which shows you how to convert your child's marks into a National Curriculum Level.

Setting the tests

Allow **45 minutes** for each of the written tests. Do not expect your child to take them one after another. In the National Test week, children will take the mathematics tests over two or three days.

For the written tests, your child will need a ruler, pencil, rubber, protractor, and, if possible, a small mirror or piece of tracing paper, together with a calculator (for Test B).

The mental test should take approximately **10–15 minutes** to give, and it is necessary for you to read aloud the questions on pages 27 to 28, which you should cut out for ease of use. Your child will only need a pencil and rubber for the mental test.

Written Tests A and B

Encourage your child to work systematically through each test, returning later to questions which cause difficulty.

If your child has difficulty in reading the questions, you can read them aloud, provided the mathematical words are not altered or explained. Where necessary, your child can dictate the answers and these can be written down for him or her. For large numbers, however, your child should be clear which digits are intended to be written, e.g. for a number such as three thousand and six, your child should indicate that this is written as three, zero, zero, six.

The Mental Maths Test

The mental test contains a series of questions for you to read to your child together with a sheet for written answers. Allow only the time suggested for each question, reading each one twice.

Marking the tests

Next to each question in the written tests is a number indicating how many marks the question or part of the question is worth. Enter your child's mark into the circle above the mark, using the answer pages to help you decide how many points to award.

Find your child's total score from the written tests and mental test and refer to page 37 for information about the level your child might be working at.

Practice Pages

Once your child has completed the tests, he or she can move on to the Practice Pages for the opportunity to boost his or her skills even further.

1 Write two more numbers in this diagram so that the numbers in each row and column add up to 150.

 20   100   **30**

80   70   **50**

50   **30**   **70**

2 The hundreds digits are missing from two numbers in this number sentence. Write what they could be.

 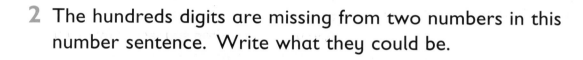 5 3 + 2 7 5 = 828

3 a Continue this sequence.

 9   16   25   36   43   52

b Explain how you worked out the missing numbers.

 _____

_____

_____

1

1

1

1

TOTAL

4

1

4 At a football tournament there are **11** players in each team.

154 players take part in the tournament.

How many teams take part in the tournament?

 11 22 33 44 55 66 77 88 99
110 121 132 143 154

14

2

5 Two of these numbers when squared are between 40 and 80.

Tick the numbers.

| 3 | 4 | 5 | 6 |

| 7 | 8 | 9 | 10 |

1

TOTAL

3

2

6 A shop sells different kinds of sandwiches. They are made with **white** bread or **brown** bread.

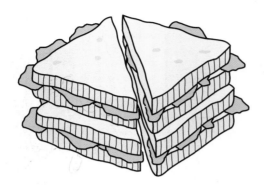

This table shows the most popular sandwiches sold in the shop during one week.

Filling	White	Brown
Bacon	9	16
Sausage	7	14
Egg	19	8

a How many **brown** bread sandwiches were sold during the week?

1

b Which filling was the least popular during the week?

1

1

7 Calculate

438 + 375

TOTAL

3

8 Mrs Jones is sending three parcels.

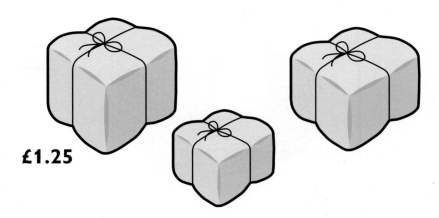

£1.25

One parcel costs **£1.25** to send. The second parcel costs twice as much.

a How much does the second parcel cost?

£1.25 × 2 = £2.50

£ 2.50

1

b Mrs Jones spends exactly £10 to send all three parcels. How much does the third parcel cost?

£3.75 + £0.25 = £6.00

£ 3.75

1

TOTAL

2

9 Playing cards come in different suits.

clubs   diamonds   hearts   spades

Here are six playing cards.

These cards are shuffled and spread out face down on a table. **One card** is picked from the set.

a What is the probability that it is a **diamond**?

Give your answer as a fraction.

1

b What is the probability that it is a **club**?

Show your answer by drawing a cross on this line.

0   1

1

TOTAL

2

10 One side of a shape has been drawn below.

The shape has **four right angles** and <u>**more than four sides**</u>.

Using a ruler, draw the other sides to complete the shape.

 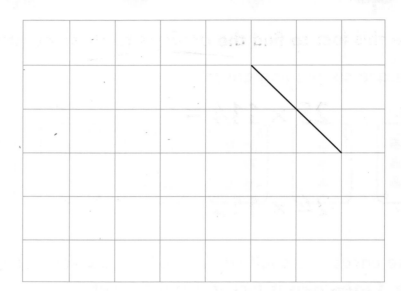

2

11 Jamie is looking at three number cards. The numbers are all different.

He notices that the **mean** of the numbers is **5**.

Write **three different numbers** that Jamie could be holding.

1

TOTAL

3

12 Look at this multiplication fact.

$$24 \times 114 = 2736$$

Use this fact to find the answers to these questions.

 a $25 \times 114 =$ 2850

1

 b $24 \times 115 =$ 2760

1

 c $240 \times 114 =$ 27360

1

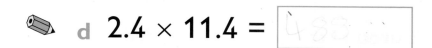 d $2.4 \times 11.4 =$ 488

1

13 Circle one fraction and one decimal that are equivalent.

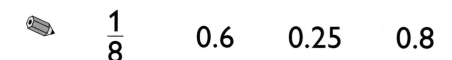 $\frac{1}{8}$ 0.6   0.25   0.8

1

0.7 $\frac{2}{5}$ $\frac{4}{5}$ $\frac{3}{4}$

TOTAL

5

7

14 a Using a ruler, mirror or tracing paper, **draw and shade** the reflection of the shape below in the mirror line.

mirror line

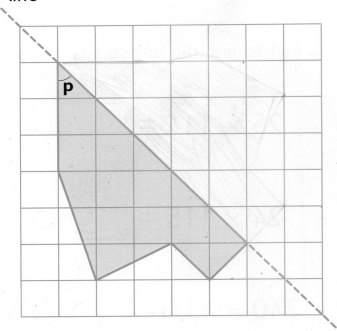

b What **area** of the grid is now shaded?

  cm²

c What **fraction** of the grid is now shaded?

d How many **degrees** is **angle p?**

You may use an angle measurer (protractor).

  180 °

2

1

1

1

TOTAL

5

8

15 Fill in the missing number so that the numbers along all three sides of the triangle have the same total.

Show your workings in the box below.

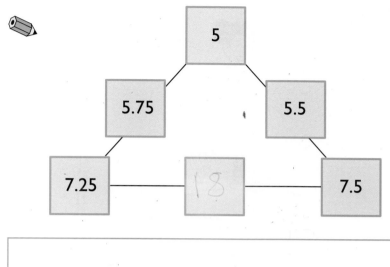

5

5.75   5.5

7.25   18   7.5

2

16 Here are two squares drawn on a graph.

Fill in the missing **co-ordinates** of **point G**.

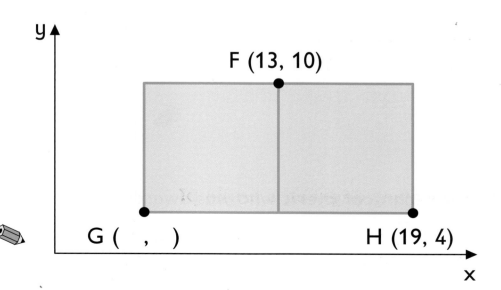

F (13, 10)

G (,)   H (19, 4)

2

TOTAL

4

17 In an ice skating competition the skaters are awarded points for **difficulty**, **style** and **technical merit**. These points are added together to find a total score.

Here are the numbers of points awarded to three children.

Name	Difficulty	Style	Technical Merit
Jo	6.4	6.7	5.8
Dev	5.7	6.3	5.2
Luke	5.6	5.7	6.3

a What is the total number of points awarded to Dev?

b For **technical merit** who was awarded **closest** to 6 points?

1

1

TOTAL

2

18 Here are some triangles that form a pattern.

The triangles are not drawn to scale.

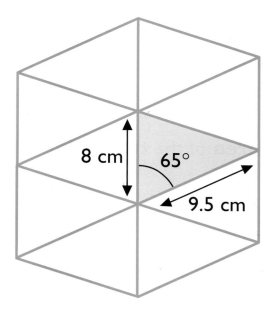

 Using a ruler and an angle measurer (protractor) draw **accurately** the shaded triangle. The vertical line has been drawn for you.

8 cm

2

TOTAL

2

19 Here are two floor tiles.

The **area** of the **square tile** is 100 cm².

The length and width of the **triangular tile** are the same as the square.

a What is the **area** of the **triangular tile**?

cm²

1

Identical tiles are arranged to cover part of a floor.

1

b What area of floor do these tiles cover?

cm²

1

c What is the length across the floor from point A to point B in **metres**?

m

TOTAL

3

20 Mr Marshall is buying some vegetables.

The vegetables come in bags of different sizes. This table shows the prices of the different bags.

	Carrots	Onions	Peppers
1.5 kg	£1.30	£1.10	£2
2 kg	£2.50	£1.40	£2.60

Mr Marshall buys **one** bag of **carrots**, **one** bag of **onions** and **one** bag of **peppers**.

He buys a total of **5.5 kg** of vegetables.

He pays **£6.20**.

Which three bags does he buy?

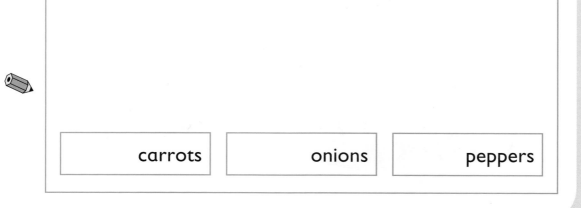

carrots   onions   peppers

2

TOTAL

2

1 Write three numbers to make the number sentence correct.

$$\boxed{} + \boxed{} + \boxed{} = 105$$

2 An arrow is pointing to each of the number lines below.

In each circle, write the number indicated by the arrow.

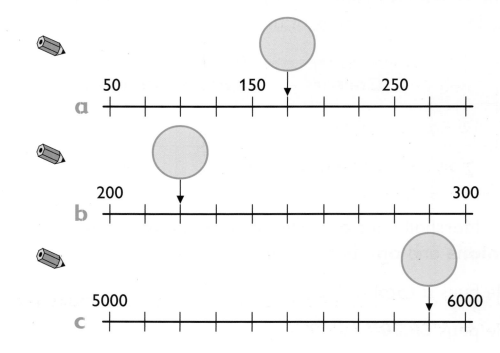

3 Use all of these digits to make the four-digit number closest to 3000.

TOTAL

5

14

4 Here are some number riddles.

Write the number for each riddle in the box.

a

> The number is between 20 and 30.
>
> It is a multiple of 3.
>
> It is a multiple of 6.
>
> It is a multiple of 8.

1

b

> The number is between 20 and 50.
>
> It is a square number.
>
> It is an even number.

1

5 Write what the **missing numbers** could be to make the number sentences correct.

 a × ☐ × ☐ = 24

1

 b ÷ ☐ = 6

1

1

TOTAL

 c 13 + 6 − ☐ = 10 + ☐

5

6 On a TV Pop Star programme, **2653** people phone in to vote. Each call costs **£3.50**.

a What is the total cost of the phone calls?

 £ [ ]

You can also vote by text message. Each text costs **95p**.

Pop Star 2013 – Vote now!

Texts cost a total of **£553.85**.

b How many text messages are sent?

1

2

TOTAL

3

16

7 This table shows the **number of kilometres** between some cities in the United Kingdom.

	Aberdeen	Cardiff	Exeter	Leeds	Newcastle
Aberdeen	–	859	946	529	380
Cardiff	859	–	196	385	515
Exeter	946	196	–	471	601
Leeds	529	385	471	–	155
Newcastle	380	515	601	155	–

a Explain why some boxes in the table do not contain numbers.

_____

_____

_____

1

A lorry driver wants to visit three cities on the same journey. He starts at **Aberdeen**, drives to **Newcastle** and then on to **Cardiff**.

b How far does he travel?

km

2

TOTAL

3

8 Here is an arrangement of dots. Join some of these dots with straight lines to draw a **regular octagon**.

Use a ruler.

○ 1

9 Jamie is laying a pattern of coloured floor tiles.

The pattern he is laying has **rotational symmetry**. He still has **one coloured tile** to lay.

Shade the square where he will lay the **coloured tile** so that the pattern will have **rotational symmetry**.

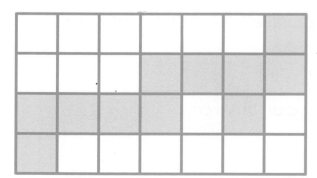

○ 1

TOTAL

○

2

10 Alison is a vet.

This table shows the hours she must work each week.

Mondays to Wednesdays	8.30 a.m. to 4 p.m.
Fridays and Saturdays	4 p.m. to midnight
1st Sunday in each month	2 p.m. to 4 p.m.

a Is Alison working at 12.30 p.m. on a Tuesday?

| yes | no |

1

b Which **day** in **every** week does Alison **not** work?

1

c Kevin says to Alison:

"You have about 50 days off work each year."

Is he correct?

| yes | no |

1

Explain your answer.

_____

_____

TOTAL

3

11 This number sequence is made by counting on in steps of **equal size**.

Fill in the **missing numbers**.

 | **14** | | | **35** | |

1

12 Here is the calendar for October 2007.

October 2007						
Sun	Mon	Tues	Weds	Thur	Fri	Sat
						1
2	3	4	5	6	7	8
9	10	11	12	13	14	15
16	17	18	19	20	21	22
23	24	25	26	27	28	29
30	31					

Jack's birthday is on **October 20th**.

In 2007 he had a party on the **Sunday after** his birthday.

a What was the **date** of his party?

1

Mia's birthday is on **November 9th**.

b On what **day of the week** was her birthday in 2007?

1

TOTAL

3

13 Look carefully at the shapes below.

They are not drawn to scale.

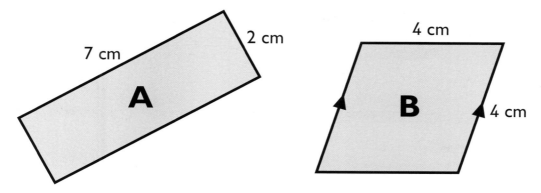

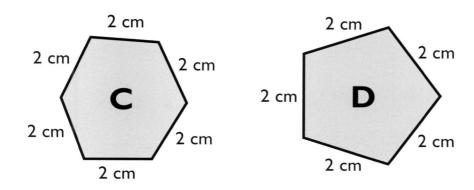

Write the letter of shapes **B**, **C** and **D** in the correct section of the table below.

Shape A has been done for you.

	Equal sides	Equal angles	Both equal sides and equal angles
Four sides		**A**	
Five sides			
Six sides			

2

TOTAL

2

14 This scale can be used for converting **litres** and **gallons**.

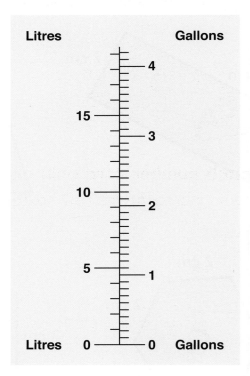

a Approximately how many **litres** are there in **3 gallons**? Give your answer to the nearest whole number.

| litres |

b Approximately how many **gallons** are there in **7 litres**? Give your answer to 1 decimal place.

| gallons |

1

2

TOTAL

3

15 Carol is arranging exactly **four** number cards to make different fractions **less than one**. These are the numbers.

a Using **each** number card only **once**, show where each would go to make this statement correct.

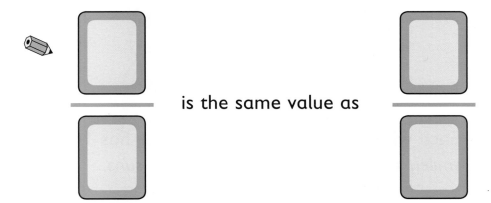

is the same value as

b Find another way to place these cards to make **different** fractions that have the same value.

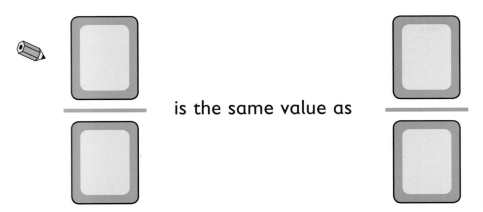

is the same value as

1

1

1

16 Calculate 12% of 850.

TOTAL

3

17 Here is part of a sheet of wrapping paper showing *smiley suns*.

Each whole sheet of wrapping paper has **14 rows** of *smiley suns*. Each row has **21** *smiley suns*.

How many **smiley suns** are there on **15** whole sheets of wrapping paper?

2

1

TOTAL

3

18 Fill in the missing number to make this statement correct.

$$15\,741 \div \boxed{} = 583$$

19 This price list shows the cost of entering a funfair and going on the rides.

Leroy pays the **entrance fee** and goes on **some rides**. He spends exactly **£2.75**.

a How many rides does he go on?

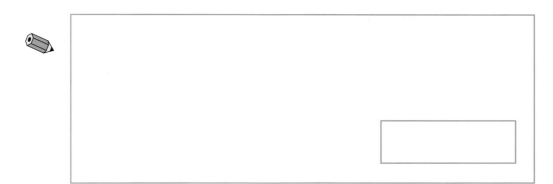

b Write a formula to show the total cost in pence (**C**) of visiting the funfair if you go on **n** rides.

  C =

1

2

TOTAL

3

20 There are **25 children** in **Class Three**.

They have been learning their times tables.

Here is a chart to show which tables the children know.

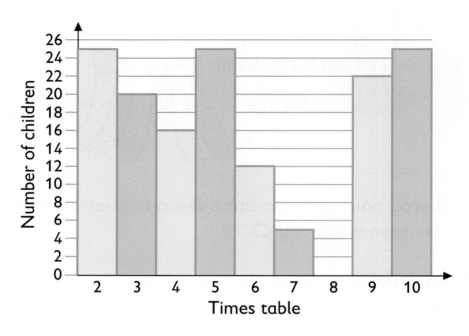

Clive says:

"More than half of Class Three know at least five of their times tables."

a Is he correct?

yes	no

Explain your answer.

  _____

_____

_____

b What **percentage** of the **25** children in Class Three know the 7 times table?

1

1

TOTAL

2

"For this first set of questions you have five seconds to work out each answer and write it down."

1 Write the number four thousand and six in figures.

2 Divide ninety by three.

3 What is six point five six multiplied by ten?

4 One-quarter of the children in a class are girls. What percentage are girls?

5 How many sides do five pentagons have in total?

6 What is double twenty-three?

"For the next set of questions you have ten seconds to work out each answer and write it down."

7 What is half of five point six?

8 How many seconds are there in three and a half minutes?

9 Add seven and seventeen and then divide by six.

10 A snail crawls sixty-three centimetres. How much further does it have to crawl to reach one metre?

11 One-quarter of a number is twenty. What is the number?

12 On the answer sheet is part of a scale. What number is the arrow pointing to?

13 A drink costs 35p. How many drinks can be bought for £3?

14 Emma walks three miles every day. How far does she walk in a week?

15 Look at the answer sheet. Draw a ring around the approximate capacity of a cup.

"For the next set of questions you have fifteen seconds to work out each answer and write it down."

16 Look at the answer sheet. Draw a ring around the number that is nearest to eight.

17 Twenty-five per cent of a number is twenty-two. What is the number?

18 Which year was nineteen years before the year two thousand and eight?

19 Look at the answer sheet. What is the size of angle C?

20 Look at the answer sheet. Draw a ring around four numbers that are multiples of nine.

5-second questions

1		4	
2		5	
3		6	

6

10-second questions

7	
8	seconds
9	
10	centimetres
11	

12		5.7 ↓ 5.8
13	
14	miles

| 15 | 300 ml   30 ml
 3 ml
 3000 ml   0.3 ml |

9

15-second questions

16	0.8 8.9 7.6 8.5 8.88
17	
18	

| 19 | C= 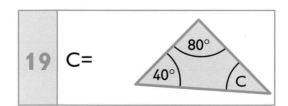 |

| 20 | 36   288   56
 106   153   108 |

5

TOTAL

20

Answers

Test A

Question number	Answer	Mark	Parent's notes and additional comments
1	100, 20	1	
2	Children should have written two digits that add to make 7, e.g. 153 + 675 253 + 575 353 + 475 453 + 375 553 + 275 or 653 + 175	1	If your child has written two digits that add to make 8, encourage him or her to add the two numbers together, e.g. 453 + 475 Point out that his or her answer comes to 928.
3a	49, 64	1	
3b	A mark for either: an explanation that the differences between numbers in the sequence go up in odd numbers (+7, +9, +11…) or increase by two each time; or a reference to "square numbers", e.g. $1 \times 1 = 1$, $2 \times 2 = 4$, $3 \times 3 = 9$, $4 \times 4 = 16$, $5 \times 5 = 25$, $6 \times 6 = 36…$	1	Children's answers to questions like these should include numbers to support their explanations. Just writing "I saw a pattern. The numbers go up" is generally not enough to score a mark. Encourage your child to learn square numbers to 100 by heart, i.e. 1, 4, 9, 16, 25, 36, 49, 64, 81, 100. They are called square numbers as these numbers of dots can be arranged to make squares, e.g. ● ●● ●●● ●●●● 　　●● ●●● ●●●● 　　　　●●● ●●●● 　　　　　　●●●●
4	14 Award 1 mark if your child has attempted to divide 154 by 11 but with an incorrect answer.	2	It does not matter whether this calculation is done mentally or using a written method.
5	7, 8	1	See note 3b for more information on square numbers.
6a	38	1	Children are required to interpret the table and then find the total of 16, 14 and 8.
6b	Sausage	1	Children should check the totals of each row to find the least popular filling.
7	813	1	
8a	£2.50 Note that amounts of money should never be written with both the £ sign and a p sign, e.g. £2.50p is incorrect and would not earn a mark.	1	Children must find twice £1.25. If they are unsure of how to do this, encourage them to double 100 and then double 25 and add the two numbers together. Children of this age should try to learn doubles of all numbers to 100 and their corresponding halves, e.g. double 75 = 150 and half of 150 = 75.
8b	£6.25	1	

Question number	Answer	Mark	Parent's notes and additional comments
9a	$\frac{1}{6}$	1	There are 6 cards. The probability of picking the only diamond is one out of six. Probabilities generally can be written in words or as fractions or decimals, e.g. **one out of four, $\frac{1}{4}$ or 0.25.**
9b		1	There are 6 cards. The probability of picking one of the three clubs is three out of six. Note that $\frac{3}{6}$ is the same as $\frac{1}{2}$.
10	Any shape with more than 4 sides and with exactly 4 right angles. 1 mark should be awarded if the shape has more than 4 sides and some right angles (but <u>not</u> exactly 4).	2	Examples of shapes: External right angles (those outside the shape) do not count.
11	Any three <u>different</u> numbers that have a total of 15, e.g. 4, 5, 6 or 2, 4, 9.	1	The mean (average) of a set of numbers is found by finding the total and dividing this by the number of "numbers" in the set. In this case there are 3 numbers so: The mean… 5 = **15** ÷ 3.
12a	2850	1	Children should notice that 25 × 114 is 114 more than 24 × 114. Ideally they should add 114 to 2736 to get 2850. A mark can be awarded if the answer was found using a different method.
12b	2760	1	Again, children should notice that 24 × 115 is 24 more than 24 × 114. If your child finds this difficult, discuss it in a context, e.g. 115 things costing £24 cost £24 more than 114 things costing £24. A mark can still be awarded if the answer was found using a different method.
12c	27 360	1	This answer is ten times larger than the given multiplication fact.
12d	27.36	1	Encourage your child to work out an approximate answer to decide where the decimal point should go, e.g. **2.4** × **11**.4 is approximately **2** x **11** = 22, so the answer is not 273.6 or 2.376, but 27.36.
13	$\frac{4}{5}$ and 0.8 are equivalent	1	Equivalent means "have the same value", e.g. if you have $\frac{4}{5}$ of a pizza it is the same amount as $\frac{8}{10}$ of a pizza, which can be written as the decimal 0.8.

Question number	Answer	Mark	Parent's notes and additional comments
14a		2	1 mark should be awarded if 4 out of the 5 corners of the shape are reflected correctly, e.g.
14b	28 cm^2	1	The area of a shape is the number of whole squares inside the shape. In this case it is centimetre squares or cm^2 that are counted. If your child gave an answer higher than 28, he or she counted half squares as whole squares.
14c	$\frac{28}{64}$ or $\frac{14}{32}$ or $\frac{7}{16}$	1	There should be 28 out of 64 squares shaded.
14d	45° Accept answers that are 1 degree either side of 45°, i.e. 44° or 46°.	1	A protractor is not essential for this question. Show your child that the angle is half a right angle and that the exact answer is 90 ÷ 2 = 45°.
15	3.25	2	All three sides should have the same total: 18.
16	(7, 4) Award 1 mark for each co-ordinate.	2	The second co-ordinate (how many up) is the same as H, i.e. 4. To work out the first co-ordinate (how far across) find the difference between 19 and 13 = 6 and then take this away from 13 to get 7.
17a	17.2	1	5.7 + 6.3 + 5.2
17b	Jo Award a mark for writing 5.8.	1	Children may incorrectly answer 6.3. Show that 5.8 is 2 tenths from 6, whereas 6.3 is 3 tenths away from 6.
18	1 mark for the angle to be between 64° and 66°. 1 mark for the length of the line to be exactly 9.5 cm.	2	Children sometimes find drawing angles using a protractor difficult when neither line is horizontal. Help them to rotate the protractor and place it appropriately. Children may also make the mistake of drawing the 9.5 cm line first and then trying to deal with the angle.
19a	50 cm^2	1	The area of the triangle is half the area of the square.
19b	2200 cm^2	1	22 whole squares each of area 100 cm^2.
19c	0.6 m Children do not score a mark for writing 60, as the answer should be in metres.	1	If a square tile has an area of 100 cm^2 then each side must measure 10 cm as 10 × 10 = 100.
20	2 kg carrots (£2.50), 1.5 kg onions (£1.10), 2 kg peppers (£2.60). Award 1 mark for attempts to add sets of three numbers, including prices and masses.	2	This question involves interpreting information and dealing with two criteria: the total price (£6.20) and mass (5.5 kg).

Question number	Answer	Mark	Parent's notes and additional comments
1	Any three numbers that add to make 105.	1	
2a	175	1	Show your child that each 100 is split into 4 sections, so each must be worth 25.
2b	220	1	Show your child that each 100 is split into 10 sections, so each must be worth 10.
2c	5900	1	Show your child that each 1000 is split into 10 sections, so each must be worth 100.
3	2931	1	
4a	24	1	A multiple is a number that can be divided exactly into without a remainder, e.g. multiples of 6 include 6, 12, 18, … 180, … 486…
4b	36	1	A square number is a number that is made from multiplying another number by itself, e.g. $4 = 2 \times 2$, $9 = 3 \times 3$, $25 = 5 \times 5$. Children should learn the square numbers to 100, i.e. 1, 4, 9, 16, 25, 36, 49, 64, 81,100.
5a	Any three numbers that multiply to make 24, e.g. $3 \times 4 \times 2$, $12 \times 2 \times 1$, $6 \times 2 \times 2$.	1	Note: $1 \times 1 \times 24$ is an acceptable answer.
5b	Any numbers that divide to make 6, e.g. $6 \div 1$, $12 \div 2$.	1	
5c	The numbers written in by the child should total 9, e.g. 4 and 5, 1 and 8, 3 and 6, or 2 and 7.	1	Children often find this type of question difficult as they see the equals sign as an "answer giver" rather than meaning "is/has the same answer as". Here $13 + 6 - \square$ "has the same answer as" $10 + \square$.
6a	£9285.50 Do **not** award a mark for the answer <u>£9285.5</u> or <u>£9285.50**p**</u>.	1	Money answers must be written correctly for questions of this type. Calculator questions like these are often selected to see whether children can interpret the display in the context of money. Amounts of money should never be written with both the **£** sign and a **p** sign.
6b	583 Award 1 mark if your child has shown that he or she is trying to divide in pounds or in pence, e.g. $553.85 \div 0.95$ or $55385 \div 95$.	2	Here children must change the amounts of money to be either in pounds or in pence. If your child has given the answer 5.83 by dividing £553.85 by 95 <u>pounds</u>, point out that the text price is given in pence and needs to be altered to £0.95.
7a	Any explanation showing that your child appreciates that the empty boxes are for distances between the same towns, e.g. Leeds to Leeds.	1	

Question number	Answer	Mark	Parent's notes and additional comments
7b	895 km Award 1 mark if the workings show 380 + 515 with an incorrect answer.	2	The most common mistake with questions of this type is to select the incorrect second distance. If your child answered 1239 km, it is because he or she used the distances between Aberdeen and Newcastle (380) and then between <u>Aberdeen</u> and Cardiff (859), rather than Aberdeen and Newcastle (380) and on from <u>Newcastle</u> to Cardiff (515).
8	A regular octagon has 8 equal sides and 8 equal angles.	1	
9	Answer →	1	Shapes or patterns that have rotational symmetry, when turned, can look the same in more than one orientation. Letters like S, H, X, O have rotational symmetry, but A, E, T, W do not. They cannot be turned to look the same in any other orientation.
10a	yes	1	
10b	Thursday	1	
10c	no Answers <u>must</u> include reference to the vet having more than one day off in most weeks and there being 52 weeks in a year.	1	Children's answers to questions like these should include <u>numbers</u> where possible, e.g. 2, 52 etc.
11	21, 28, 42	1	To answer this question children should find the difference between 35 and 14 = 21. If the difference between boxes that are three apart is 21 then the difference between each box is 21 ÷ 3 = 7.
12a	October 23 or 23-10-07 or Sunday 23rd October	1	Accept any indication that the child has recognised the date 23rd October. But do not accept incorrect dates, e.g. 23-9-07 or 21st October.
12b	Wednesday	1	
13	 Award 1 mark if all but one of the letters are correctly positioned.	2	Children will often think that Shape B (a type of parallelogram called a rhombus) has equal sides and equal angles. Use the corner of a piece of paper to show your child how two of the angles are smaller than a right angle (acute) and two are larger than a right angle (obtuse).
14a	14 litres	1	
14b	Award 2 marks for 1.5 and 1 mark for 1.6.	2	
15a	$\frac{3}{6}$ and $\frac{4}{8}$ or $\frac{3}{4}$ and $\frac{6}{8}$	1	The fractions can be in any order, e.g. $\frac{3}{6}$ and $\frac{4}{8}$ or $\frac{4}{8}$ and $\frac{3}{6}$.
15b	$\frac{3}{6}$ and $\frac{4}{8}$ or $\frac{3}{4}$ and $\frac{6}{8}$ Do <u>not</u> award a mark if the answer has the same fractions as question 15a, even if given in a different order.	1	

Question number	Answer	Mark	Parent's notes and additional comments
16	102	1	12% of 850 can be worked out in the following ways: *or* $12 \div 100 \times 850$ *or* $12 \times 850 \div 100$ *or* 850×0.12
17	4410 Award 1 mark for a method that shows $14 \times 21 \times 15$ with an incorrect answer.	2	
18	27	1	Children often attempt questions of this type using trial and error, e.g. trying to divide 15 741 by different numbers to get 583. This involves a great deal of time. Instead, encourage your child to see that division questions can be rearranged, e.g. $10 \div 5 = 2$ and $10 \div 2 = 5$. Here children should divide 15 741 by 583 to get 27.
19a	7	1	Children may incorrectly answer 9.16 or 10. Remind them that the entrance fee (65p) should be subtracted first.
19b	Any of the following answers: $C = 65 + (30 \times n)$ $C = 65 + (n \times 30)$ $C = 65 + 30n$ $C = 30n + 65$ $C = 30 \times n + 65$ etc. Award 1 mark for: $C = 30n$ or $C = 30 \times n$	2	Children find using letters in place of numbers quite difficult. Show them the following: For 1 ride C (cost) $= 65 + (1 \times 30)$ For 2 rides C (cost) $= 65 + (2 \times 30)$ For 3 rides C (cost) $= 65 + (3 \times 30)$ etc. So for n rides C (cost) $= 65 + (n \times 30)$ etc.
20a	yes There must be an explanation with references to the fact that more columns are above $12\frac{1}{2}$ than are below, i.e. more tables are known by more than half the class than are not known.	1	The 2, 3, 4, 5, 9 and 10 times tables are known by more than half the class and only the 6, 7, and 8 times tables are known by less than half the class.
20b	20%	1	Children must read the bar chart to see that 5 children know the 7 times table. They must see that there are 25 children in the class. 5 out of 25 children is 20%. This can be found on the calculator by keying $5 \div 25 \times 100$.

Answers

Mental Maths Test

1. 4006
2. 30
3. 65.6
4. 25%
5. 25
6. 46
7. 2.8
8. 210 seconds
9. 4
10. 37 cm
11. 80
12. 5.77
13. 8
14. 21 miles
15. 300 ml
16. 7.6
17. 88
18. 1989
19. 60°
20. 36, 288, 153, 108

Mark scored in Test A		out of 40
Mark scored in Test B		out of 40
Mark scored in Mental Maths Test		out of 20
Total score		out of 100

The National Tests are levelled according to the child's total score.

Mark	24 or below	25–51	52–79	80–100
Level	Level 1/2	Level 3	Level 4	Level 5

For each test this can be broadly broken down as follows:

Test A	Mark	0–10	11–20	21–31	32–40
	Level	Level 1/2	Level 3	Level 4	Level 5

Test B	Mark	0–10	11–20	21–31	32–40
	Level	Level 1/2	Level 3	Level 4	Level 5

Mental Maths Test	Mark	0–4	5–10	11–15	16–20
	Level	Level 1/2	Level 3	Level 4	Level 5

Now go on to the Practice Pages to help your child even further.

Number and Algebra

1 Calculate:

354 + 168 = ☐   496 + 544 = ☐

604 − 348 = ☐   5029 − 1174 = ☐

24 × 6 = ☐   542 × 5 = ☐

87 ÷ 3 = ☐   112 ÷ 7 = ☐

8

2 Fill in the missing signs: +, −, ×, ÷

4 ◯ 5 = 20   6 ◯ 4 = 1.5

25 ◯ 5 = 20   12 ◯ 14 = 26

15 ◯ 5 ◯ 2 = 12

27 ◯ 9 ◯ 8 = 24

6

3 Use this fact

$$112 \times 22 = 2464$$

to write down the answers to:

112 × 23 = ☐   113 × 22 = ☐

112 × 220 = ☐   1.12 × 2.2 = ☐

4

TOTAL

18

Number and Algebra

4 Fill in the missing numbers.

$24 \div \boxed{} = 6$

$7 \times \boxed{} = 49$

$29 - 10 = 16 + \boxed{}$

$(5 \times 2) + 17 = 30 - \boxed{}$

4

5 Continue and explain these patterns:

3, 6, 9, 12, $\boxed{}$ $\boxed{}$

_____

_____

23, 19, 15, 11, $\boxed{}$ $\boxed{}$

_____

_____

4

1, 3, 6, 10, 15, $\boxed{}$ $\boxed{}$

_____

_____

100, 81, 64, 49, $\boxed{}$ $\boxed{}$

TOTAL

8

_____

_____

Number and Algebra

6 Fill in the missing numbers.

$$7836 + \boxed{} = 10\,001$$

$$\boxed{} - 416 = 838$$

$$8 \times \boxed{} = 552$$

$$11\,697 \div \boxed{} = 21$$

$$\boxed{} \times 43 = 559$$

$$\boxed{} \div 34 = 39$$

7 Answer these word questions.

97 children are going by car on a trip. Four children can go in each car. How many cars are needed?

$$\boxed{} \text{ cars}$$

How many 17 cm lengths of string can be cut from a length of 4 m?

$$\boxed{} \text{ lengths}$$

I have 68 pence. How many 8p chews can I buy?

$$\boxed{} \text{ chews}$$

6

3

TOTAL

9

Number and Algebra

8 Circle two equivalent fractions in each row.

$$\frac{1}{2} \qquad \frac{2}{3} \qquad \frac{3}{4} \qquad \frac{1}{4} \qquad \frac{3}{5} \qquad \frac{6}{8} \qquad \frac{7}{10}$$

$$\frac{1}{3} \qquad \frac{5}{6} \qquad \frac{7}{9} \qquad \frac{3}{4} \qquad \frac{3}{6} \qquad \frac{4}{5} \qquad \frac{1}{2}$$

$$\frac{8}{10} \qquad \frac{2}{3} \qquad \frac{1}{4} \qquad \frac{1}{6} \qquad \frac{4}{5} \qquad \frac{4}{8} \qquad \frac{4}{10}$$

3

9 Which of these questions has an answer nearest to 4?

$3.42 \times 1.5 = $ ☐ $2.4 \times 1.2 = $ ☐

$1.42 \times 2.5 = $ ☐ $2.2 \times 2.2 = $ ☐

1

10 Answer these percentage questions.

Find 25% of each of these numbers.

80 ☐   100 ☐   240 ☐   12 ☐

8

Find 75% of each of these numbers.

80 ☐   100 ☐   240 ☐   12 ☐

2

What is: 15% of 80? ☐

12% of 250? ☐

TOTAL

14

Shape, Space and Measures

11 Reflect this shape in the mirror line.

mirror line

p

1

12 Answer these questions about the grid.

How many degrees is angle p?

What area is now shaded?

What area is now unshaded?

3

13 Measure and label these angles with an angle measurer (protractor).

1

A

B

C

TOTAL

5

Shape, Space and Measures

14 The minute hand turns clockwise on a clock.

Give the angles it turns between these pairs of numbers.

From 12 to 3	☐	From 3 to 9	☐
From 9 to 10	☐	From 10 to 12	☐
From 12 to 9	☐	From 9 to 1	☐
From 1 to 5	☐	From 5 to 12	☐

8

15 Here are some start and finish times of TV programmes.
How long does each programme last?

	Start	Finish	Length of programme
Comedy	6:30	7:00	
Film	8:15	9:45	
Soap	11:35	12:00	
Drama	12:30	13:45	
Documentary	14:20	15:15	
Travel	16:32	17:05	
News	18:18	18:29	
Wildlife	19:34	20:28	

8

TOTAL

16

Answers

Practice Pages

1. 522   1040
    256   3855
    144   2710
    29 16

2. ×   ÷
    −   +
    −, +
    ÷, ×

3. 2576   2486
    24 640   2.464

4. 4
    7
    3
    3

5. 15, 18
These are multiples of 3. The difference between adjacent numbers is 3 each time.
7, 3
The difference between adjacent numbers is 4 each time. The pattern is going down (decreasing) by 4 each time.
21, 28
The difference between adjacent numbers is going up 1 each time. The pattern is going +2, +3, +4, +5... These numbers are called triangular numbers.
36, 25
These numbers are called square numbers, 10×10, 9×9, 8×8 ...

6. 2165
    1254
    69
    557
    13
    1326

7. 25
    23
    8

8. $\frac{3}{4}$ and $\frac{6}{8}$
    $\frac{3}{6}$ and $\frac{1}{2}$
    $\frac{8}{10}$ and $\frac{4}{5}$

9. $1.42 \times 2.5 = 3.55$

10. 20   25   60   3
     60   75   180   9
     12
     30

11.

12. p = 45°
     19 cm^2
     45 cm^2

13. A = 38°
     B = 55°
     C = 104°

14. 90°   180°
     30°   60°
     270°   120°
     120°   210°

15. 30 minutes
     1 hour 30 minutes
     25 minutes
     1 hour 15 minutes
     55 minutes
     33 minutes
     11 minutes
     54 minutes